**6 Studies
for Groups or Individuals
with Notes for Leaders**

Peter Scazzero

New Life in Christ

the discipleship series

ZONDERVAN™

GRAND RAPIDS, MICHIGAN 49530 USA

ZONDERVAN™

New Life in Christ
Copyright © 1992 by Peter Scazzero
All rights reserved

Requests for information should be addressed to:
Zondervan, *Grand Rapids, Michigan 49530*

ISBN 0-310-54761-X

Edited by Jack Kuhatschek
Interior design by Ann Cherryman

Printed in the United States of America

04 05 06 07 /❖ CH/ 20 19 18 17 16 15 14 13

Contents

The Discipleship Series

Welcome to The Discipleship Series, a unique new program designed with one purpose in mind—to make you a stronger, more effective disciple of Jesus Christ.

Whether you are a new Christian, a newly committed Christian, or someone who simply wants a deeper walk with God, The Discipleship Series can help you reach your goal of spiritual maturity.

You'll be learning from people who are known for their wisdom and godly example. The authors of this series are not armchair theologians, but seasoned veterans who have been disciples and disciplemakers for many years. Step by step they will guide you through the essentials of what it means to follow Christ and to become more like him.

The Discipleship Series is designed to be flexible. You can use the guides in any order that is best for you or your group. They are ideal for Sunday-school classes, small groups, one-on-one relationships, or as materials for your quiet times.

Because each guide contains only six studies, you can easily explore more than one facet of discipleship. In a Sunday-school class, any two guides can be combined for a quarter (twelve weeks), or the entire series can be covered in a year.

Each study deliberately focuses on a limited number of passages, usually only one or two. That allows you to see each passage in its context, avoiding the temptation of prooftexting and the frustration of "Bible hopscotch" (jumping from verse to verse). If you would like to look up additional passages, a Bible concordance will give the most help.

The Discipleship Series helps you *discover* what the Bible says rather than simply *telling* you the answers. The questions encourage you to think and to explore options rather than merely to fill in the blanks with one-word answers.

Leader's notes are provided in the back of each guide. They show how to lead a group discussion, provide additional information on questions, and suggest ways to deal with problems that may come up in the discussion. With such helps, someone with little or no experience can lead an effective study.

Suggestions for Individual Study

1. Begin each study with prayer. Ask God to help you understand the passage and to apply it to your life.

2. A good modern translation, such as the *New International Version,* the *New American Standard Bible,* or the *New New Revised Standard Version,* will give you the most help. Questions in this guide, however, are based on the *New International Version.*

3. Read and reread the passage(s). You must know what the passage says before you can understand what it means and how it applies to you.

4. Write your answers in the space provided in the study guide. This will help you to clearly express your understanding of the passage.

5. Keep a Bible dictionary handy. Use it to look up any unfamiliar words, names, or places.

Suggestions for Group Study

1. Come to the study prepared. Careful preparation will greatly enrich your time in group discussion.

2. Be willing to join in the discussion. The leader of the group will not be lecturing but will encourage people to discuss what they have learned in the passage. Plan to share what God has taught you in your individual study.

3. Stick to the passage being studied. Base your answers on the verses being discussed rather than on outside authorities such as commentaries or your favorite author or speaker.

4. Try to be sensitive to the other members of the group. Listen attentively when they speak, and be affirming whenever you can. This will encourage more hesitant members of the group to participate.

5. Be careful not to dominate the discussion. By all means participate! But allow others to have equal time.

6. If you are the discussion leader, you will find additional suggestions and helpful ideas in the leader's notes at the back of the guide.

Introducing New Life in Christ

A cartoon I once saw showed a chicken egg, standing on end. Suddenly, the egg started to wobble from side to side, and a crack began to encircle the top half. Finally, the egg burst open, and a baby chick poked his head upward. As he blinked at his new surroundings, the chick exclaimed, "I *knew* there must be more to life!"

When we become Christians, we break free from our dark confines and become aware of a bright new reality. Martin Luther, the great Protestant reformer, describes how he experienced this new life after reading Romans 1:17: "I felt myself to be reborn and to have gone through open doors into paradise. The whole Scripture took on new meaning, and whereas before the 'righteousness of God' had filled me with hate, now it became inexpressibly sweet in greater love. This passage in Paul became to me a gateway to heaven."

Yet our new life in Christ is much more than what we experience at conversion. Just as a child is filled with awe and wonder at seeing snow for the first time or catching his first fish, so we must become alert to seeing all that God has given us in Christ.

A story in the Old Testament describes how Elisha's servant woke up one morning and was terrified to discover that the city was surrounded by a foreign army. "'Oh, my lord, what shall we do?' the servant asked.

'Don't be afraid,' the prophet answered. 'Those who are with us are more than those who are with them.'

And Elisha prayed, 'O Lord, open his eyes so he may see.' Then the Lord opened the servant's eyes and he looked and saw the hills full of horses and chariots of fire all around Elisha" (2 Kings 6:15–17).

In a similar way, the apostle Paul wrote: "I pray also that the eyes of your heart may be enlightened in order that you may know the hope to which he has called you, the riches of his glorious inheritance in the saints, and his incomparably great power for us who believe" (Ephesians 1:18–19).

The purpose of this study guide—*New Life in Christ*—is to help you grasp the hope, the riches, and the great power God has given us through his Son. Whether you are a new Christian or one whose eyesight has dimmed with age, there is far more to experience than you (or I) have ever imagined.

Peter Scazzero

John 3:1–18

Welcome to the Family

In his famous allegory, Pilgrim's Progress, *John Bunyan describes a man named Christian, who searches for a way to get rid of the burden of sin on his back. He meets a man named Evangelist, who tells him to flee the City of Destruction (his home town) and pass through the narrow gate leading to eternal life.*

As he leaves for the gate outside the city, his wife, children, neighbors, and friends mock and cry after him not to go. Nonetheless, he puts his fingers to his ears, runs across the plain to the gate, and cries: "Life! Life! Eternal Life!" When he passes through the small gate, the burden of sin on his back rolls away, and he begins the journey to heaven, the City of God.

When you made that momentous decision to surrender your life to Jesus Christ, you began a journey filled with exciting surprises!

A rich variety of biblical metaphors are used to describe what has happened to you. You are a plant that needs nourishment and care in order to grow and bear fruit (Colossians 2:6–7). You are an athlete running a race God has specially marked out for you (1 Corinthians 9:24–27). You have been supernaturally born a second time by the Holy Spirit. And you have entered the kingdom of God (John 3:3–8).

In John 3 Jesus uses the image of a baby's birth to describe the beginning of the Christian life. In this study we want to grasp Jesus' powerful explanation of this miracle.

1. What events and circumstances led you to decide to follow Jesus?

2. Read John 3:1–18. What can you discover about Nicodemus from verses 1–4 and 9–12?

3. Nicodemus was a member of the Jewish ruling council, the Sanhedrin. This was the group of seventy elders with religious and moral authority over the entire Jewish nation. Why do you think Nicodemus comes to see Jesus (v. 2)?

4. For a religious leader like Nicodemus, the only requirement to enter the kingdom of God was to be a law-abiding, physically-born Jew. In light of this, why do you think Jesus abruptly introduces the subject of the new birth?

What problem does this immediately pose for Nicodemus, and why (v. 4)?

5. Jesus is talking about two kinds of births—natural and spiritual. In your own words, explain Jesus' response to Nicodemus (vv. 5–8).

6. Why is the wind such a vivid image of the way God's Spirit invades our lives (v. 8)? (Note: The Greek word for "wind" and "spirit" is the same.)

In what ways has the wind of the Holy Spirit transformed your life?

---

7. Why is *new birth*—not simply right intellectual beliefs or good works—absolutely essential for entering God's kingdom?

---

8. Nicodemus' question (v. 9) reveals that he still doesn't understand the mystery of being born "from above." How might his life change if he were to accept Jesus' testimony (v. 11) and be born again?

---

9. How does Moses' lifting up a snake on a pole correspond to Jesus being lifting up on the cross (vv. 14–15; see Numbers 21:4–9)?

How does this illustration apply to our need today and Jesus' offer? (Consider: the personal needs in both incidents, God's provision in both, and the response necessary for salvation.)

10. According to verses 15–18, what are the only two alternatives and consequences for each person in the human race?

11. What impresses you most about God's supreme act of love for you (vv. 16–17)?

12. Paul wrote: "Therefore, if anyone is in Christ, he is a new creation; the old has gone, the new has come!" (2 Corinthians 5:17). What does it mean for you that the old things have passed away and all things have become new? (Be specific.)

13. Spend time worshiping God for the way he opened your eyes and gave you a new life!

Memory Verse

Therefore, if anyone is in Christ, he is a new creation; the old has gone, the new has come!

2 Corinthians 5:17

Between Studies

The gospel. Look up the following verses, noting what you learn about God, ourselves, and Jesus:

❑ God (Genesis 1:27; John 10:10; Romans 1:18; 1 John 1:5)

❑ Humanity (Isaiah 53:6; 59:2; Romans 3:23; 6:23)

❑ Jesus (Romans 5:8; 1 Corinthians 15:3–4;
   1 Timothy 2:5)

❑ **Response** (Acts 2:38; John 1:12; Revelation 3:20).

Your testimony. Use the outline below to describe how you came to Christ. Share this good news with someone this week.

1.   What I was like before I became a Christian:

2.   What God used to open my eyes (people, circumstances, and so on):

3. How I came to know Christ (what aspect of the gospel touched me):

4. How Christ has changed my life since that time (relationships, goals, attitudes, desires):

John 15:1–17

Getting to Know Jesus

I once saw a cartoon that pictured a large supercomputer that had stopped working. An army of technicians was climbing all over the computer, opening panels, checking circuits, and making sophisticated tests. The reader, however, could see what the technicians had failed to notice—the computer was unplugged!

As Christians, we often engage in a flurry of activities to promote our spiritual growth. We go to church regularly, become active in ministry, attend seminars, and then wonder why our relationship with Jesus seems shallow and superficial. Yet we may overlook the obvious—we have neglected the One who is the source of our life.

In John 15, Jesus lays down principles for how we can know him better and become fruitful disciples.

---

1. What are some obstacles—either people or circumstances—that hinder your spiritual growth?

2. Read John 15:1–17. How does Jesus describe the relationship between himself and his followers (vv. 1–8)?

3. How would you describe the goal or purpose of our relationship with Jesus (vv. 1–4, 8, 16)?

What does it mean for you, in practical ways, to bear fruit (see also Galatians 5:22–23)?

4. Like a gardener, the Father prunes us so that we will become more fruitful (vv. 2–3). What pain might be associated with pruning?

In what ways do you sense God "pruning" areas of your life so that you might be like Jesus?

5. In addition to bearing fruit, what other promises flow out of remaining in Jesus (vv. 4, 7, 8, 11, 16)? (Note at least three.)

6. Jesus' repeated command is "remain in me." What do you think that means?

7. It is easy to have a superficial relationship with the vine, giving the *appearance* of being connected (for example, going to church and saying the right words). But what is the result of trying to follow Jesus without having intimate communion with him (vv. 4–6)? Explain.

8. What are some practical ways you can develop intimacy and communion with the Lord Jesus?

9. What is the relationship between our remaining in Jesus' love and our loving each other (vv. 9–13)? Explain.

10. What are some practical ways we can lay down our lives for each other (vv. 12–13)?

11. According to Jesus, how does our relationship with him go beyond servant and master (vv. 14–15)?

12. How does the relationship between a servant and master contrast with that between two friends?

How should these differences affect our relationship with Jesus?

13. The vine metaphor dramatizes our need to remain united to Jesus in a life-sustaining relationship. While it is important to talk with Jesus throughout the day, it is also good to set aside a special time each day to be alone with him (see Luke 4:42). What changes would you need to make in your schedule to spend fifteen to thirty minutes a day with Jesus in the Word and prayer?

Memory Verse

I am the vine; you are the branches. If a man remains in me and I in him, he will bear much fruit; apart from me you can do nothing.

John 15:5

Between Studies

Make a commitment to spend fifteen to thirty minutes with Jesus each day this week. In order to make this time as effective as possible, you will need to do the following:

❑ Pick a time when you can be alone, free from interruptions and distractions.

❑ Choose a place that is both quiet and comfortable.

❑ Begin your time by reading and meditating on a passage of Scripture, such as a psalm.

❑ Go to the Lord in prayer. One simple but helpful way to guide your prayers is to remember the acronym ACTS:

A=Adoration
C=Confession
T=Thanksgiving
S=Supplication*

Recommended reading: *Intimate Moments with the Savior* and *Incredible Moments with the Savior* by Ken Gire (Zondervan).

Supplication means praying for your needs and those of others.

Acts 2:41–47
Ephesians 4:1–16

Finding Strength in God's Family

Commitment in relationships is out. The divorce rate is climbing, with half of all new marriages ending in divorce. While there is a deep yearning for close, open relationships, adults today feel they have fewer close friends than people did in past decades.*

In fact the world has been compared to a massive flock of sea gulls—individualists, selfish, cruel, and often fighting among themselves.

Geese, on the other hand, are found to possess the opposite qualities. They fly in V formation with the point goose bearing the wind. The point goose is rotated every few minutes. The strongest goose then permits the oldest and weakest geese to fly in back. If one goose becomes sick or tired and is forced to drop out, a strong goose drops out with him. A goose is never abandoned. Not only does this cooperation help their well-being and survival, it enables them to fly 71% faster than the individualist sea gulls!

---

*George Barna. *The Frog in the Kettle* (Ventura, Calif.: Regal Books, 1990), 34.

In contrast to the "sea gull"-like world in which we live, Christians are called to a radical love and commitment to each other. If you want to experience spiritual wholeness and maturity, you must have authentic, biblical relationships with other brothers and sisters in Christ.

---

1. At what moments in your life have you sensed the most unity (for example, on an athletic team, in the army, in a sorority or fraternity, in your family)? Explain.

---

2. Read Acts 2:41–47. In the book of Acts we are given a glimpse into the early days of the church. What one or two things impress you about this church as you read about it?

To what four things did they continually devote themselves?

---

3. In contrast to modern society where "every man is out for himself," what is so shocking about their life together (vv. 44–46)?

Imagine yourself both as a new Christian and a new member of this church. What kinds of things might you see, experience, hear, or feel?

---

4. What were the results of the believers' deep commitment to each another?

---

5. The word *fellowship* comes from the Greek word *koinonia*. This rich word refers to sharing, participating, being intimate together. It implies community and interdependence. In what practical ways can you devote yourself to "the fellowship"?

---

6. Read Ephesians 4:1–16. What qualities does the apostle Paul urge us to demonstrate in our life together (vv. 1–2)?

Why are these character qualities important for maintaining unity with each other—especially if we have varying economic and educational backgrounds?

7. How does Paul's description of the body of Christ, the church, motivate us to love each other and live in unity (vv. 4–6)?

8. Verses 7–10 describe Jesus as a conquering hero who leads a triumphal procession and distributes gifts—the fruit of victory—to his followers. What are the purposes and goals of these gifts (vv. 11–13)?

9. How do you think an infant in Christ would behave differently from a mature believer (v. 14)?

10. How do our relationships in the body of Christ affect our growth from spiritual infancy to maturity (vv. 15–16)?

11. What practical steps can you take to function more effectively in the body of Christ?

In what ways can you demonstrate love to another believer this week?

Memory Verses

A new command I give you: Love one another. As I have loved you, so you must love one another. By this all men will know that you are my disciples, if you love one another.
John 13:34–35

Let us not give up meeting together, as some are in the habit of doing, but let us encourage one another—and all the more as you see the Day approaching.
Hebrews 10:25

Between Studies

Read 1 Corinthians 12:12–26, reflecting on your place in the family of God.

Using the chart on the following page, contrast life in the kingdom of God and the world. Look up the verses for those items in the column on the right.

The World	The Kingdom of God
Save your life	Lose your life (Mark 8:35)
Get, get, get	Give and it will be given to you (Luke 6:38)
Hold grudges	Forgive as the Lord forgave you (Colossians 3:13)
Don't let anyone step on you	Humble yourself and ask forgiveness (1 Peter 5:6; Matthew 5:23–26)
Be Number One	The last shall be first (Mark 10:31)
Lead	Serve (John 13:12–17)
Keep up an image	Confess your sins to one another (James 5:16)
Criticize, gossip	Let no unwholesome word go out of your mouth (Ephesians 4:29)
Don't tell the truth; it will only make things worse	Speak the truth in love (Ephesians 4:15)
Hate your enemy	Love your enemy (Matthew 5:44)
Retaliate; get even	Do not repay anyone evil for evil (Romans 12:17)
Spend time with the beautiful, the accepted, the rich	Invite the poor, crippled, blind, and lame to your house (Luke 14:13–14)
Give up on people when they disappoint you	Love always perseveres (1 Corinthians 13:7)

Acts 2:1–21
John 16:5–15; 7:37–39

Being Filled with the Spirit

The story is told of a woman who had served the Queen of England faithfully for many years. At retirement she was given a scroll which read, "Entitled to all the Wealth of the Royal Family," so that she could live comfortably the rest of her life. Since the old woman could not read, she simply framed the scroll and hung it on her wall. The result: she lived in abject poverty! Years later a friend discovered the scroll on the wall, explained to her the wealth to which she was entitled, and she lived happily ever after.

This woman's story illustrates the way some believers live. They are entitled to great wealth but live poorly.

God has provided all the power and strength you need to follow Jesus and enjoy the spiritual wealth he purchased for you at the cross. The way to experience these spiritual riches is through a proper relationship with the Holy Spirit. In this study we will consider how the Holy Spirit can strengthen, guide, and change you.

1. Before you became a Christian, what was the driving force or controlling power in your life?

2. Read Acts 2:1–21. Following his resurrection, Jesus commanded the disciples to wait in Jerusalem for the coming of the Holy Spirit (Acts 1:4–8). For ten days the believers prayed together and waited (1:14). Then came the great Jewish feast of Pentecost. What is the order of events on the day of Pentecost (2:1–4)?

3. What immediate effect does the Spirit have on the disciples and the crowd that gathers (vv. 3–13)?

4. How does Peter explain the events taking place before their eyes (vv. 14–21)?

5. Prior to the coming of Jesus, the Holy Spirit came only upon kings, prophets, priests and judges. On what kinds of people does the Holy Spirit now come (vv. 17–18)?

What are some of the results we can expect (see also Acts 1:8)?

6. Read John 16:5–15. When Jesus announces that he is going away, how do the disciples feel, and why (see also vv. 20–22)?

7. In what ways is it better for us to have the Holy Spirit actively present than to have Jesus physically here on earth?

8. The word "Counselor" (sometimes translated "Comforter," "Helper," "Advocate") refers to the Holy Spirit (14:26). What three functions will the Holy Spirit carry out when Jesus goes away (vv. 8–11)?

In what ways did you experience these activities of the Holy Spirit *before* your commitment to Jesus?

9. How does Jesus explain the Holy Spirit's ministry *after* we become believers (vv. 12–15)?

Why do you think verse 14 is often called the heart of the Holy Spirit's ministry?

10. Read John 7:37–39. What condition and steps does Jesus lay down for being filled with the Spirit?

11. What hindrances in your life (pride, resentment, and so on) might quench your thirst?

12. What is Jesus' promise, and what can we expect?

13. Take a few moments and surrender your life afresh to Jesus, telling him you are thirsty and asking him to fill you with the Holy Spirit.

Memory Verses

But you will receive power when the Holy Spirit comes on you; and you will be my witnesses in Jerusalem, and in all Judea and Samaria, and to the ends of the earth.

Acts 1:8

If you then, though you are evil, know how to give good gifts to your children, how much more will your Father in heaven give the Holy Spirit to those who ask him!

Luke 11:13

Between Studies

Ask God to fill you with the Holy Spirit each day (Ephesians 5:18). Pray that you will hear his voice and sense his promptings throughout the day.

Ask the Lord to set up "divine appointments" for you, so that you can be his witness this week (Acts 1:8).

Recommended reading: *Introducing Jesus* by Peter Scazzero (IVP) helps you learn how to share Christ with your friends through investigative Bible studies. *I Believe in the Holy Spirit* by Michael Green (Eerdmans).

Ephesians 6:10–20

Resisting
the Enemy

In the 1980s a young German teenager named Brian Rust shocked the world when he piloted a small single-engine airplane from Denmark and flew into some of the most heavily guarded airspace in the world. He landed in Red Square, the center of Moscow, outside the General Secretary's office and Lenin's tomb. The Soviet Union's military was so strong and determined that they considered it impossible for an "invader" to fly in undetected. Yet the naivete of the USSR left them unaware of an opening in their air defense system.

As a Christian you are engaged in a war with a supernatural enemy. He is determined not only to penetrate your "spiritual airspace" but also to terminate your relationship with Jesus Christ.

Any country at war spends millions of dollars studying their enemies so they are not caught off guard. Spiritual warfare likewise demands that we know our enemy so that we can resist his attacks.

---

1. In what ways have you sensed that you are in a spiritual battle as a Christian? Explain.

2.   Read Ephesians 6:10–18. According to verse 12, what is the ultimate cause of evil and trouble in the world today?

How is that different than the way most people (and even many Christians) view reality?

3.   What four categories of demonic powers does Paul describe in verse 12?

How does Paul urge us to resist these demonic powers (vv. 10–11)?

4. Four times Paul exhorts us to stand firm in our war against the devil's schemes (vv. 11–14). What are some ways you are susceptible to spiritual defeat?

5. Paul uses the illustration of a Roman soldier in verses 13–18. What might happen to a soldier who entered battle without all his armor (or modern-day equipment)?

6. The belt of a soldier was to be buckled tightly around the waist. This way an enemy couldn't grab it. Why is "the belt of truth" (v. 14) essential for success in spiritual battles?

7. The breastplate was a metal chestplate that protected a soldier from stabs, arrows, and punches. The "breastplate of righteousness" (v. 14) refers to both our right standing in Jesus Christ and to our right living. How can you ensure that you put on this "breastplate" each day?

8. The footgear of a Roman soldier was both protective and supportive. Why do you think feet fitted and ready with the gospel of peace form a part of our spiritual armor? (See also Romans 10:15.)

9. Archers used fiery arrows against their enemies before making a frontal assault. The soldier's shield was his primary protection from these arrows. Why is the "shield of faith" (v. 16) so essential for us in battle?

In what way(s) has a fiery dart from the evil one recently rained down on you (for example, false guilt, doubt, fear, pride, discouragement)?

10. The soldier's helmet was made of heavy metal and was able to ward off the blows of even a three- to four-foot club! How can the "helmet of salvation" (v. 17) equip you against the blows of the enemy?

11. Why are the "word of God" and prayers "in the Spirit" (vv. 17–20) the only offensive weapons we need in battle?

12. Which piece of armor do you need most today as you seek to follow Jesus? Explain.

Memory Verses

For our struggle is not against flesh and blood, but against the rulers, against the authorities, against the powers of this dark world and against the spiritual forces of evil in the heavenly realms.

Ephesians 6:12

For God did not give us a spirit of timidity, but a spirit of power, of love and of self-discipline.

2 Timothy 1:7

Between Studies

Prepare yourself for battle. For the next week begin each day by reviewing this passage and putting on your spiritual armor, piece by piece:

Belt of truth (v. 14)	What passage of Scripture can you meditate on throughout the day?
Breastplate of righteousness (v. 14)	Realize your position in Christ (Romans 8:1) and confess any known sin to God.
Feet fitted with the gospel of peace (v. 15)	Ask the Holy Spirit to open up a door for you to share Jesus with someone.
Shield of faith (v. 16)	What fiery dart might be coming at you today? Pray, putting up the shield of faith.
Helmet of salvation (v. 17)	Rejoice in the fact that he who began a good work in you will carry it on to completion until the day of Christ Jesus (Philippians 1:6).
Sword of the Spirit (v. 17)	Ask God to bring to life specific portions of Scripture that will enable you to do battle.
Pray in the Spirit on all occasions (v. 18)	Draw near to God in prayer each day.

Recommended Books: *This Present Darkness* by Frank Perretti (Crossway). This will give you a fresh way of looking at the world around you. *Spiritual Warfare* by George Mallone (IVP). A good introduction to this theme.

Luke 14:25–34
Matthew 13:44–46

Following Jesus

Abraham Lincoln was a man who knew what it meant to persevere. He failed in business (1831). He was defeated for the Legislature (1832). He failed again in business (1833). While deeply in love, his fiancee died (1835). He suffered a nervous breakdown (1836). He was defeated for Speaker of the Legislature (1838). He was defeated for Congress (1843). He was defeated again for Congress (1848). He was defeated for the Senate (1855). He was defeated for Vice President (1856). He was defeated again for the Senate (1858). Finally, he was elected President of the United States (1860).

Lincoln faced continual pressures and disappointments, yet he was able to press on to his ultimate task of serving the nation. While Jesus Christ does not call us to failure and defeat, he does call us to persevere in following him.

For this reason the Bible compares us to athletes who, having undergone strict training, are to run in such a way as to get a prize (1 Corinthians 9:24–27). Scripture also compares us to soldiers enduring hardship in the midst of a war, calling us to avoid entangling ourselves in the affairs of civilian life (2 Timothy 2:3–4). Finally, we are compared to farmers, whose hard work in the fields earns them the first share of a crop (2 Timothy 2:6).

In Luke 14 and Matthew 13, Jesus himself describes what it costs to be his disciple.

1. Satan has often been called the author of discouragement. What are some of the things that could discourage you from following Jesus?

2. Read Luke 14:25–34. What is shocking about Jesus' words to the crowds in verses 26–27?

What does such strong language indicate about how Jesus views these "followers"?

3. In this context "hate" (v. 26) is a common Hebrew exaggeration to make a point (see Matthew 10:27 and 15:3–4 where Jesus tells us to honor our parents). How then is Jesus asking us to view our family and our life?

4. A person carrying a cross in the first century was on his way to crucifixion. In light of what the cross meant for Jesus, what does it mean for us to "carry our cross" (v. 27)?

5. Why do you think Jesus makes such hard statements?

6. How does Jesus' first story (vv. 28–30) illustrate the types of costs involved in building a tower?

7. How does the story about the king (vv. 31–33) illustrate the cost of following Jesus?

8. What are some of the costs of following Jesus for you? (Be specific, considering such areas as money, time, career, relationships, school, goals, family, and so on.)

9. How does Jesus finally summarize his "tough sermon" in verse 33?

What difference should Jesus' words make in the way we view and handle our material wealth?

10. Salt, in New Testament times, was used to promote life (either as a fertilizer or in food) and to resist corruption. How do these two purposes illustrate what a Christian's influence in the world should be like (vv. 34–35)? Explain.

11. How are people who follow Jesus on their own terms, or only superficially, like salt that has lost its saltiness?

12. Jesus is referred to as "Lord" in the New Testament. In what areas of your life is Jesus not yet Lord? (Consider your career/job, attitudes, money, relationships, family, and so on.) Explain.

13. Read Matthew 13:44–46. What causes the two men in the two stories to respond with such emotion and energy?

What do these two parables teach about the value of the kingdom (that is, living under Christ's rule)?

14. The famous missionary C. T. Studd once said: "If Christ be God and died for me, what sacrifice can I make for Him that would be too great?" How does his statement help us keep the "cost of discipleship" in proper perspective?

Memory Verse

If anyone would come after me, he must deny himself and take up his cross and follow me. For whoever wants to save his life will lose it, but whoever loses his life for me and for the gospel will save it.

Mark 8:34–35

Between Studies

What steps can you begin to take to strengthen Christ's lordship over the following areas of your life?

❏ Your family:

❏ Your other relationships:

❑ Your job/career:

❑ Your money and possessions:

❑ Your attitudes:

❑ Your body:

❑ Your leisure time:

Recommended Reading: *The Magnificent Obsession* by John White (IVP). (Formerly *The Cost of Commitment.*)

Leader's Notes

Leading a Bible discussion—especially for the first time—can make you feel both nervous and excited. If you are nervous, realize that you are in good company. Many biblical leaders, such as Moses, Joshua, and the apostle Paul, felt nervous and inadequate to lead others (see, for example, 1 Corinthians 2:3). Yet God's grace was sufficient for them, just as it will be for you.

Some excitement is also natural. Your leadership is a gift to the others in the group. Keep in mind, however, that other group members also share responsibility for the group. Your role is simply to stimulate discussion by asking questions and encouraging people to respond. The suggestions listed below can help you to be an effective leader.

Preparing to Lead

1. Ask God to help you understand and apply the passage to your own life. Unless that happens, you will not be prepared to lead others.

2. Carefully work through each question in the study guide. Meditate and reflect on the passage as you formulate your answers.

3. Familiarize yourself with the leader's notes for the study. These will help you understand the purpose of the study and will provide valuable information about the questions in the study.

4. Pray for the various members of the group. Ask God to use these studies to make you better disciples of Jesus Christ.

5. Before the first meeting, make sure each person has a study guide. Encourage them to prepare beforehand for each study.

Leading the Study

1. Begin the study on time. If people realize that the study begins on schedule, they will work harder to arrive on time.

2. At the beginning of your first time together, explain that these studies are designed to be discussions, not lectures. Encourage everyone to participate, but realize that some may be hesitant to speak during the first few sessions.

3. Read the introductory paragraph at the beginning of the discussion. This will orient the group to the passage being studied.

4. Read the passage aloud. You may choose to do this yourself, or you might ask for volunteers.

5. The questions in the guide are designed to be used just as they are written. If you wish, you may simply read each one aloud to the group. Or you may prefer to express them in your own words. Unnecessary rewording of the questions, however, is not recommended.

6. Don't be afraid of silence. People in the group may need time to think before responding.

7. Avoid answering your own questions. If necessary, rephrase a question until it is clearly understood. Even an eager group will quickly become passive and silent if they think the leader will do most of the talking.

8. Encourage more than one answer to each question. Ask, "What do the rest of you think?" or "Anyone else?" until several people have had a chance to respond.

9. Try to be affirming whenever possible. Let people know you appreciate their insights into the passage.

10. Never reject an answer. If it is clearly wrong, ask, "Which verse led you to that conclusion?" Or let the group handle the problem by asking them what they think about the question.

11. Avoid going off on tangents. If people wander off course, gently bring them back to the passage being considered.

12. Conclude your time together with conversational prayer. Ask God to help you apply those things that you learned in the study.

13. End on time. This will be easier if you control the pace of the discussion by not spending too much time on some questions or too little on others.

Many more suggestions and helps are found in the book *Leading Bible Discussions* (InterVarsity Press). Reading it would be well worth your time.

Study One

Welcome to the Family
John 3:1–18

Purpose: To grasp the meaning and implications of what it means to become a Christian.

Question 1.

Every study begins with an "approach question," which is discussed *before* reading the passage. An approach question is designed to do three things.

First, it helps to break the ice. Because an approach question doesn't require any knowledge of the passage or any special preparation, it can get people talking and can help them to warm up to each other.

Second, an approach question can motivate people to study the passage at hand. At the beginning of the study, people in the group aren't necessarily ready to jump into the world of the Bible. Their minds may be on other things (their kids, a problem at work, an upcoming meeting) that have nothing to do with the study. An approach question can capture their interest and draw them into the discussion by raising important issues related to the study. The question becomes a bridge between their personal lives and the answers found in Scripture.

Third, a good approach question can reveal where people's thoughts or feelings need to be transformed by Scripture. That is why it is important to ask the approach question *before* reading the passage. The passage might inhibit the spontaneous, honest answers people might have given, because they feel compelled to give biblical answers. The approach question allows them to compare their personal thoughts and feelings with what they later discover in Scripture.

Question 2.

It is interesting that Nicodemus comes to see Jesus "at night," especially after Jesus cleansed the temple in chapter 2! You might want to ask the group *why* they think Nicodemus came at night.

Question 4.

Nicodemus is astonished by Jesus' demand that you *must* be born again to enter the kingdom of God. The kingdom of God refers to coming under the rule of God. Before we put our faith in Christ, the Bible describes us as belonging to the kingdom of darkness and running our own lives (Colossians 1:12). When we turn to Jesus by faith, we submit to his rule.

Jesus' point is clear: Entry into the kingdom of God is not by human striving (John 1:12) but is something only God can do. With this one statement Jesus topples all Nicodemus's understanding of how to get right with God.

Question 5.

There are two primary interpretations of the phrase "born of water and the Spirit" (v. 5). One popular view is that "water" refers to natural birth in a mother's womb. The point then is that Nicodemus must be born both naturally and of "the Spirit."

The context of the book, however, points to the ministry of John the Baptist. Water represents repentance and purification, as in John the Baptist's "baptism of repentance" (Mark 1:4). His ministry was still in process.

Nicodemus needed to enter into all that John's purifying water symbolized as well as receiving the Holy Spirit. (See also Ezekiel 36:25–26.)

"Water denotes the baptism of John into (i.e., preparing for) Jesus" (George Beasely Murray, *John,* Word Biblical Commentary [Waco, Tex.: Word, 1987], 49). Baptism in water and the Spirit becomes in the book of Acts the way of initiation into the Christian community. "Repent and be baptized, every one of you, . . . and you will receive the gift of the Holy Spirit" (Acts 2:38). Nicodemus can't be a secret disciple. He represents those who believed in Jesus but were afraid to confess him (2:23–25; 12:42). The point is not that baptism is necessary for salvation, or that a person is born again through baptism. Rather, true faith requires a willingness to be publicly joined with the people of God.

You may want to use this moment to talk about baptism as an important step of obedience once you've been born again into the kingdom of God. But don't get sidetracked and miss the heart of what Jesus is saying.

Be careful to focus on Jesus' main point—we receive the new birth by faith. It is something God does by the Spirit. We can't understand it. It is mysterious and invisible. The *effect* of God's breathing on us, however, like wind blowing over us, is observable.

Question 9.

This is a vivid picture of what Jesus has done for us on the cross (God's provision), our need (dead in our sins), and the necessary response of faith for life. Depending on the amount of time you have available in the study, help the group enter into what Jesus is saying here. It will make John 3:16 come alive in a whole new way.

Jesus refers to himself eighty-one times as the "Son of Man" in the New Testament. This messianic title describes his character and mission in terms of the vision described in Daniel 7:13-14 as "one like a son of man, coming with the clouds of heaven. . . . His dominion is an everlasting dominion."

Questions 12–13.

Be sure to allow time for these application questions, giving people opportunity to express what God has done for them.

Study Two

Getting to Know Jesus
John 15:1–17

Purpose: To understand the nature of our personal relationship with Jesus Christ and to take concrete steps toward establishing a daily time with him.

Question 3.

For further Scripture concerning God's purpose for us see also Ephesians 2:10 and Romans 8:29.

Question 7.

Judas is an example of a fruitless branch. He was with Jesus for three full years and appeared to be a branch attached to the vine. He was, however, fruitless and without life, never really having the life of Christ in him.

Question 8.

In question 13 this study will introduce the discipline of a daily "quiet time." There are, however, many other ways to encourage remaining in Christ. Brother Lawrence's *Practicing the Presence of God* is an insightful study of how to spend all day in the presence of God, whether at work or play. Fellowship with other believers is another. Fasting, taking one-day or half-day retreats, worshiping, and keeping a journal are others. Books such as *Celebration of Discipline* by Richard Foster and *Ordering Your Private World* by Gordon MacDonald are also helpful.

Questions 11–12.

Be sure to impress on the group the difference between servants and friends. Friends are partners, not slaves. Jesus shares with us and speaks with us. We are called to become his intimate friend. Some people in your group may have difficulty relating to Jesus this way, preferring to see him only as their Master, Judge, and Lord. While these are true, the thrust of the New Testament is that we can now approach God as Father or "Daddy" (Romans 8:17; Galatians 4:4). This should drive us to spend time with him.

Question 13.

As a follow-up to this question, encourage the group to do the Between Studies project. It gives them practical advice on how to have an effective time alone with the Lord.

Study Three

Finding Strength in God's Family

Acts 2:41–47
Ephesians 4:1–16

Purpose: To give an understanding of the importance of God's family, so that each member of the group will seek to relate biblically to each other.

Question 2.

Note carefully that their commitment to Christ immediately resulted in a commitment to each other as the body of Christ. The Greek word for "devoted" (v. 42) means literally "were continually devoted," implying a depth of commitment and perseverance.

The believers had common meals together "from house to house." This included the frequent "breaking of bread"; that is, the celebration of the Lord's Supper together (see 1 Cor. 11:17–34). Note also that they met in each other's homes in a spirit of intense and sincere joy! (See I. Howard Marshall, *Acts*, Tyndale New Testament Commentaries [Grand Rapids, Mich.: Eerdmans, 1980], 84–85.)

Question 5.

You may need to help new believers with this question. Help them get a vision for God's church in the midst of a sinful world, shining as a light on a hill. If appropriate, remind them that the early church was full of sinful, flesh-and-blood people like us with weaknesses, blind spots, character flaws, and annoying habits—just as you will find in any church today! It even included people who were hypocrites (see Acts 5). Yet out of devotion to Christ, the early Christians were devoted to each other.

At the same time, God's call for us is to be *in* the world but not *of* the world (John 17:15–17). Encourage the group to develop healthy, authentic friendships with other believers, while maintaining their witness with their non-Christian friends.

Question 6.

To appreciate the practical difficulty the early church had in maintaining fellowship, remember that Jews regarded Gentiles as "heathen dogs." William Barclay writes: "The Jew had an immense contempt for the Gentile. The Gentiles, said the Jews, were created by God to be fuel for the fires of hell. . . .

The barrier between them was absolute. If a Jewish boy married a Gentile girl, or if a Jewish girl married a Gentile boy, the funeral of that Jewish boy or girl was carried out. Such contact with a Gentile was the equivalent of death" (quoted in John Stott's, *The Message of Ephesians* [Downers Grove, Ill.: Inter-Varsity Press, 1979], 91).

Question 11.

This is an excellent place to go into the nature and purpose of spiritual gifts. Depending on where the group is spiritually, you may want to encourage them to reflect on 1 Corinthians 12:12–28.

Study Four   Being Filled with the Spirit

Acts 2:1–21
John 16:5–15; 7:37–39

Purpose: To consider how the Holy Spirit can strengthen, guide, and change us.

Question 2.

Be careful not to get sidetracked into a discussion of being baptized with the Holy Spirit versus being filled with the Holy Spirit. This event is called the baptism with the Holy Spirit in Acts 1:5, but Acts 2:4 also says they were "filled with the Holy Spirit." The key point you will want to make here is that to "be baptized with the Holy Spirit" (Acts 1:5; 11:16) is the same as the initial filling the disciples received at Pentecost. The verb "baptize," however, is never used for the repeated experience. Yet a person "filled" with the Spirit can receive a fresh filling for a specific task (see Acts 4:8). Paul also urges us to be continually filled with the Spirit (Ephesians 5:18–20).

Question 3.

Believing Jews went to Jerusalem for three main feasts a year: Passover, Pentecost and the Feast of Tabernacles. At Pentecost, therefore, Jerusalem was filled with Jews and Gentiles from all over the Middle East and the Roman Empire who had converted to Judaism.

Most spoke Aramaic and Greek. Yet each Jew had a native language that almost no one else knew. The crowds were astonished to hear these men from a small province in Palestine called Galilee speaking their languages.

Question 4.

Peter regards Joel's prophecy (Joel 2:28–32) as being fulfilled before their very eyes. The last days had now begun because the Spirit was being poured out on all people, with signs and wonders following, so that everyone might call on the Lord and be saved.

Questions 6-7.

To the disciples, Jesus' departure seemed disastrous. Yet Jesus knew that the presence and ministry of the Holy Spirit were of such value that it was for their good!

Question 8.

When John says the Holy Spirit will "convict the world of guilt in regard to sin and righteousness and judgment," he is referring to the Spirit's ministry of exposing people's true spiritual condition and convicting them of the truth about Jesus. The "prince of this world" refers to Satan, who was defeated at the cross. As a result, we can trust the Holy Spirit to go before us in our evangelism.

Questions 11–13.

There are four important verbs in John 7:37–38—*thirst, come, drink,* and *believe.* While every believer receives the Holy Spirit at conversion (Ephesians 1:13; Romans 8:14), we still thirst and must come regularly to Jesus to receive the fullness of the Spirit. Don't get hung up on terminology about baptism of the Holy Spirit versus fullness of the Spirit or being filled with the Spirit. As Billy Graham has noted, the key is not that we get our labels straight, but that we get the power the church experienced in the book of Acts.

You may find David Watson's testimony of being filled with the Spirit helpful: "I had a glass there in my hand, but I was not drinking and not believing. Eventually God opened my eyes and gave me the gift of faith to believe the promise I had known so well—the promise of Jesus in Luke 11:13: 'How much more will the heavenly Father give the Holy Spirit to those who ask him!' I said, 'Lord, I believe now; and I believe that I shall receive now, and I will start praising you that you have now met my need, you have filled me now with your Holy Spirit.' And as I started to praise him I had a most wonderful, quiet sense of joy and peace in the Lord. The precise nature of the experience is not important; it differs with different people. But we need to trust that as we come to Jesus and ask for this fullness of the Spirit, this power for witnessing for Him, that He means what He promises."[*]

Study Five   Resisting the Enemy

Ephesians 6:10–20

Purpose: To understand the nature of spiritual warfare and how to apply the armor of God in daily life.

Question 2.

C. S. Lewis once remarked that "there are two equal and opposite errors into which our race can fall about devils. One is to disbelieve in their existence. The other is to believe, and to feel an excessive and unhealthy interest in them." Our

---

[*]David Watson, *How to Win the War* (Wheaton, Ill.: Shaw Publishers, 1972), 145.

problem in the twentieth century is that we are largely unaware that we are in spiritual warfare.

Satan is identified by a number of descriptive names in the Bible. He is called the prince of the power of the air, the great red dragon, the god of this world, the accuser, and a roaring lion. His one goal is to rob God of his glory, and so he seeks to destroy the work and the people of God. He is responsible for blinding people to the light of the gospel (2 Corinthians 4:3–4) and is the ultimate cause of all misery in the world (John 10:10).

Paul's thrust is that we need to see the powers of darkness at work behind the scenes in our communities, cities, countries, cultures, and world in order to see as God sees.

To give us a biblical picture of the kind of warfare we are in, Paul writes: "Our struggle is not against flesh and blood" (v. 12). "Struggle" comes from the Greek word for "wrestling." It refers to intimate, hand-to-hand combat with an enemy. That is how real God desires spiritual warfare be to us.

Question 3.

The Bible indicates that God has an organization of holy angels (with archangels, cherubim, and seraphim—each with different functions). At the same time there appear to be distinctions and ranks among demons. Paul describes them as rulers, authorities, powers of this dark world, and spiritual forces of evil in the heavenly realms.

We get a glimpse of spiritual warfare in Daniel 10:2–3 and 12–14 when Daniel is in prayer. His prayer releases an angel from God's presence. On the way, however, the angel meets resistance from "the prince of Persia," a powerful demonic spirit. For twenty-one days a battle is waged in the heavens until the persistent prayer of Daniel enables the angel to break through. While you don't want the group to get sidetracked on this issue, you should seek to communicate the biblical truth of the awesome warfare that is going on around us in the heavenly realms.

Question 5.

Remember, we are called to put on the full armor, not a part. The church has many wounded, fearful soldiers who have dropped out of battle because they were not fully dressed. Nonetheless, God calls us to conquer. He has given us all the defenses we need for protection and all the weapons we need for victory.

Question 8.

The Word of God, prayer, and worship (2 Chronicles 20 and Acts 16:19–31) have traditionally been seen as our offensive weapons in spiritual warfare. I believe, however, that the shoes fitted with the gospel of peace—in other words, evangelism—should also be included in this list. Evangelism changes us. It changes the very spiritual atmosphere of an area. Finally, it changes the person who hears the Word. For this reason Satan tries to keep us from sharing our faith with power and consistency.

Question 9.

Each piece of armor is worth an entire study by itself. Spend a few minutes, however, applying this question and helping the group use the shield of faith.

Question 10.

You may wish to remind the group that salvation has three aspects: (1) past: I have been freed from the penalty of sin; (2) present: I am being increasingly set free from the power of sin (also referred to as sanctification); (3) future: I will be with Jesus one day forever and ever—sinless and with a new body.

Question 11.

The sword referred to here was six to eighteen inches long and was used for hand-to-hand combat. Jesus used this weapon to resist Satan's attack during his temptation in the wilderness (Matthew 4:1–11).

Study Six   Following Jesus
Luke 14:25–34
Matthew 13:44–46

Purpose: To understand what it costs to follow Jesus and to evaluate our lives in light of his lordship.

Question 3.

Jesus' point is that loyalty to him must take precedence over all other relationships. He must have first place.

Question 4.

Crucifixion involved losing your life. Jesus said: "For whoever wants to save his life will lose it, but whoever loses his life for me will save it" (Luke 9:24). It means putting to death your goals, plans, ambitions, and sinful desires in order to live for Jesus.

Questions 7–8.

It is important to help believers think through the decision they have made about following Jesus. Every Christian encounters opposition and discouragement. Jesus wants us to think through what his followers face so we will not be surprised and say: "But I thought I had signed up for the abundant life of John 10:10," or "I came for peace in my heart and forgiveness, not battle!" Abundant life, peace, and forgiveness are all true and part of the gospel. Yet Jesus wants us to have a more complete picture of what biblical discipleship entails.

Question 9.

Be careful not to fall into the extreme of either literally applying or over-spiritualizing Christ's words so that the group misses his point. Christ does not demand that every believer give away everything. Although he does make this demand with the rich young ruler (Luke 18:18–29), he does not with Zacchaeus the tax collector (Luke 19:1–10). The point is that following Christ means having truly renounced the god of materialism and the hold it has on our lives. As citizens of the kingdom of God, we can say with Paul, "I have learned the secret of being content in any and every situation" (Philippians 4:12). This will be seen clearly toward the end of the study when Matthew 13:44–46 is considered.

Questions 13–14.

These parables of the kingdom of God are crucial to a balanced understanding of the cost of discipleship. The motivation for obedience to Christ's lordship is a vision of his beauty and glory. God desires that we become so enthralled with his grace—having found that pearl and treasure—that all else has little value in comparison. When we are filled with love for Jesus Christ, it takes little effort to give up the world's trivial pleasures!

We want to hear from you. Please send your comments about this book to us in care of zreview@zondervan.com. Thank you.

GRAND RAPIDS, MICHIGAN 49530 USA

WWW.ZONDERVAN.COM